The Craving of Knives

To Jannie:
Many thanks for the reading venue and for the trade of books.

Blaine Marchand

blaine
Edmonton Poetry Festival
April 23, 2015

BuschekBooks
Ottawa

Library and Archives Canada Cataloguing in Publication

Marchand, Blaine, 1949-
The craving of knives / Blaine Marchand.

Poems.
ISBN 978-1-894543-58-3

I. Title.

PS8576.A633C73 2009 C811'.54 C2009-906174-0

---

cover image: Knife and paper, istockphoto
file # 7260278

Printed in Winnipeg, Manitoba, Canada by Hignell Book Printing.

BuschekBooks
P.O. Box 74053, 5 Beechwood Avenue
Ottawa, Ontario, Canada K1M 2H9
www.buschekbooks.com

BuschekBooks acknowledges the support of the Canada Council for the Arts which last year invested $20.1 million in writing and publishing throughout Canada.

Canada Council for the Arts Conseil des Arts du Canada

This book is in memory of Anne Szumigalski, poet and dancer extraordinaire, who chided me the last time I saw her for not pursuing my poetic abilities; and

for Jamie Robertson, my life line.

"Before the brain, before its language, there is nothing we can tell each other, nothing beyond the here and now. The dark describes what we fear most; not the unknown, but what we fail to recognize."

"Maps Of All We Have Been"
Immune To Gravity
Mary di Michele

Table of Contents

4.

1.

First Taste

This was my first taste of it:
age four or five,
up there, in the newsreel
on the big screen
of the drive-in theatre,
beyond the inclined heads
of my sister and her boyfriend,
through the reedy voice
in the speaker
hooked onto the window,
sounding like my friend
through the tin can with string,
and the car was filled
with pungence of nearby mown hay,
and my hand was in the popcorn,
and up there, soldiers kept
opening doors
to ovens, to showers, to dormitories,
and they were everywhere,
pale as popcorn,
and they were thrown into pits,
the bodies a nest of grubs
my friend that day had
squashed with his heel,
and my hand was in the popcorn
and this was my first taste of it.

The point

We were vaguely aware,
which added to the thrill.
But this was the point
in the bay where squared timber
booms, chained together, breached
through the water, wide as sidewalks
over which our naive feet rushed.

From the rocks, we dove to explore
murky depths, the bloated deadheads
and creviced millstones settled
in the silt, deep holes where it was said
giant muskie waited to lunge and maim.

We swam against the current,
through rapids to logjams knotted
as nerve ends. We unbraided
these twined puzzles then rode the final
log, hollering and gulping,
our obscured feet towing
against the pin ends
of broken shale
as the current
drew us down.

Each summer, it finally hit home.
We huddled on the shore
while men pushed out in a boat,
held our breath as the hook
beat like a fist through water,
snagged its prey, a drowned boy.

Wildfire

1

the boy runs through shadows,
imagines burnt logs strewn
across pavement. he leaps
over the charred embers. his heart
in his mouth. the afternoon air
scalding his nostrils,
throat seared
as if he had drunk acid.

what is he running from,
this boy with wildfire feet?
why does fear
shiver him?
monsters lurk
in the gulf between houses,
lie in wait in the
dense shrubbery,
ready to pounce.

this morning awakening,
dreams were shards
in his skin, the curtain,
a coiled serpent. a blot of crow stained
the fabric as it flew
from the tree just outside
his window. later, he turned
away from the mirror,
hypnotized by water wrenched down
the sink. the boy held his breath,
waited, convinced a hand
would reach up, pull
him through, that voice
in the loop had gargled
his name.

2

this morning, when her arm stretched out,
the boy closed his eyes, thought
soft down of parakeet, feathers
fluffing the air as the puff
that flounced her skin. he wanted
to nestle against her,
unfold into her
perfumed clothes.

he opened his eyes
but her fingers were rotating the dial.
a match flared. the gas
hissed a blue tongue. he leaned toward
her, longing
for the heat of her hand
against his cheek, the whisper
of cotton as she moved.

a pot rasped across the coil
of element. he waited,
listening for the water
to bubble, for the porridge, slow
as his brain, to simmer,
mouths opening,
closing across its surface,
breathing. he was hungry. starved
for sounds, for cereal
to fill him up, for her touch.

3

last night, the blonde wood gleamed
in the lamp's spilt milk.
the tv in front
of the window and beyond
in the indigo sky, the skull
of moon between the ears
of antenna. her fingertip had traced
the edge of the console, snapped open
its doors, turned the knob
and a glow of embers infused
the screen. she left the room.
an image focused: a baby
crying in a woman's arms
who rocked and rocked,
brought her lips
to its forehead. the baby
shrieked. her hand
brushed back a strand
of errant hair, rubbed
her forehead. the baby wailed.
the boy covered his ears
but his eyes were held.
the woman twisted,
lifted the burner
of a woodstove. flames
cracked into the air.
the woman leaned forward.
the baby's head
entered the hoop of flame.

Grosbeaks

Grey flannels chafe my legs;
shoes, like shiny pebbles, pinch my toes.
I shuffle back and forth
between my mother and father,
drag red rosary beads with a clatter
down the pew. My father coughs;
my mother's hand stills
mine; and Father Bambrick's hairy fist
makes the pulpit thunder. I startle.
His thick index finger jabs the air.

"*Once there was a man who questioned eternity.*
One day he fell asleep only to wake,
find everything he loved gone.
His wife dead, his children vanished,
his house fallen into ruin."

Father Bambrick's callused palms
rise toward heaven. A ray of sunlight
illuminates the golden thread heart, pierced
by arrows, embroidered on his purple chasuble.

This morning as I wake
yellow grosbeaks are caged
by the wiry branches of the rowan,
bills heavy with last year's wizened berries.
The sun smolders the peaks of houses,
burnishes the birds with goldleaf.

Last night you said a child's worry
is not death but eternity.
The child in me grows smaller,
yet that terror remains,
its voice more frantic.

The birds, like sparks, spiral
beyond the cremation of darkness;
they drop the fruit,
hearts impaled by blades of grass.

The man with the golden mouth

1

such thirst
the wind curdles the dust
above the savannah
my tongue in my mouth
circles, suppliant
a dance to bring
moisture from clouds

a young African urinates
his flow a cataract
he turns to see
if I am watching

later as I stand beside the car
he lifts his shirt,
skin dark mud,
drags a finger up under the hem
of his shorts, asks
where I am staying,
my address back home

I move away,
my silence a protection,
as the glass through which I watch,
am watched, welcoming
the distance, (me here,
him, thirty paces apart),

and thankful for the ocean
that will separate us,
aware desire's undertow
fills me with dread

2

my father's mouth
sewn shut, the tumour in the jaw
cut away and his hands
lashed to the bedframe
his eyes wide, a frightened animal,
the words my father so often wanted
to say lodged under his tongue.
my father, raised
on an ideal of perfection, the right
thing to do, saving
face, and me,
his son overwhelmed,
powerless, my fingers
covering my mouth
wanting to offer him
water, comfort, and unable

to run from his sight

3

who is that man with the golden mouth?
teeth laced together with wire,
in cross-stitch, fine as embroidery on white linen

his lip curled as the curve
his car took too tightly.
Not for him
the straight and narrow
but defiance. Head tilted back,
throat tremulous with scorn,
sun coruscating the waves in his hair,

he speaks through clenched teeth,
takes nourishment from a straw angled
into the gap. One hand straddles his hip,
legs firmly apart
rock him back and forth in his boots
worn as creviced wood, the mangled
steel he stepped from, dust, blood
the taste of life in his mouth

who is that man and why
do I want
to stand so close, believing
his brute force will scour
me to words?

Compulsion

1

I can't remember what he said
just the fine silver wire
his right hand drew from his left
as if he were a sorcerer
pulling a thin blade of knife
from under his skin

I saw his mouth moving
but was pinned by the press
of his torso, the force of metal
against the curve of my neck,
its bite about to pierce
the artery.

The breath words expelled
through his teeth stank
but I was mesmerized by the spurt
of blood, the crash of his
heart against my fist of ribs

then a surge of anger
drove my arms
to lift him, throw him
two stories to an atrium below.

I tried to recall what he said
as my feet pummeled down steps
to a door that was locked,
its embedded mesh blurring
my view of the crowd
that cradled his body, bore it away.

I was certain his words were the key.
my knees gave way, I crashed to the floor.
Anguish burst from my mouth as
an other man's hands cradled
my father's face.

2

No, this is all lies.
It was not as vivid
as this retelling,
these images were conjured
much later
from some dark snare
of my imagining.

The truth lies
in the dread on re-opening
my eyes, the banality
of my bedroom, sheets tossed
to one side, room cold
as a wake,
and the nagging
question hounding me
through the hours as relentless
digits sifted across the clock.

Yes, he seemed my father,
his words were ever so clear
though days, weeks, years later,
as I flip the memory
open, a switchblade
in my hand, the words hold
no substance and leave me
burdened as winter night
is bled through by daybreak.

3

This compulsion to fabricate
contrive, invent—
I am a child trembling,
needing my shadows,
ghosts lurking behind doors,
my words in absence of his.

It seemed the form of my father
but was not him.
I will say it honestly
—it was a fear of my own making
but why, even now,
I do not fully comprehend
just as the artery,
ignored until now,
twitches below the surface of my skin
and I imagine it
potent with blood.

The craving of knives

The knives are no longer content.
You notice it in the way
they sink their teeth into
lobes of bread,
leave marks as they slice
open the hearts of tomatoes.

For years they seemed so happy,
performing without complaint
the ritual preparation of red meat,
the deboning of fish.
They have allowed
themselves to be pitted against
whetstone by a brutal hand;
they have remained mute,
slotted into racks when no longer needed.
Only recently have they even permitted
their tension
to be taken up
by the grip on their handles.

Such acknowledgement has made them
all the more desperate
to spill out their rich vocabulary
of anger and pain.
Each one wants to spit it out,
open mouths
along wrists, across necks.

It has led to such rivalry among them.
Only one will be selected
to leave its mark
on the sheets and in the bathtub.
Only one.
And they are frantic,

certain the real reasons
will be misunderstood.
The chosen one
picked up,
tagged as merely the weapon.

The tumult of waves

These trees are twisted, perched
on the edge of Juan de Fuca
Strait, battered by winds that pivot
and turn, anger exploding,
fists raining down. They lean away

in terror from the crumbling
cliff, which plunges down
to the beach, where men in wetsuits
step onto boards, clutch bars curving
round sails translucent as a shaving of skin.
Caught in the tumult of waves, the men
lose control, are flung into the air,
across water as if they were stones.

In the distance, the Olympics brood,
an apparition like the face of God, smug
with pretext, rise above clouds.
The sun, setting, strews a bloody net
into a cove where a mummified tree,
a once elegant hand, lies severed.

Void

All night long, drifting
in and out of sleep. The fan
a hand trying to lift my skin.

Earlier, in a crypt
the ancient tour guide bent down,
with thumb and forefinger
raised a leathery flap
of stomach, the remains
of an old Coptic nun at peace
for 500 years. Inside,
her kidneys, liver, spleen brown
as stones that the ocean deposits
in a hidden bay.

All night long,
a young black girl, the empty basket
of her eyes crusted with rheum,
fingers exploring
her cavity of mouth,
nearby, a Tureg man in a jade turban,
flicking up the lid
of a camel-hide coffer,
inside, boxes dyed
maroon, emerald, ebony,
hollow
spaces in a sunken chest

All night,
vendors swarm in market streets
tugging at my shoulders, arms, wrists
a knife slicing open a chest.

I can't breathe

All night
drift in and out
unsettled,
searching for
somewhere inside,
a void
where I can be
mortared, brick by brick.

2.

The Pale Object of Desire

Sleep weights the body,
like the Rift Valley wall,
between sheets and cover.
At the deepest point,
the moon floats above the rim.
Sometimes ridged fingers
of an inclined hand.
Sometimes the pale plain
between a rise of hip bones.
Sometimes hair drifting
across a face.

Deep within the body
desire is an ancient land
nomads wander through
and never possess;
is a water catchment
drawn to the surface,
of the parched savannah.

The tropic sun
slides under the eyelids,
dissolves.
But traces remain,
stippled with moisture.
Morning light whets
the canopies of acacia,
douses the leafless baobabs
like hairs on the folds
of far-off hills,
like the down matted
at the torso's divide.

Precipice

I always think of you when flying
over the foothills west of Calgary.
How they erupt, break through the earth,
push their jagged peaks into the air,
a foetus no longer willing to be contained,
or the way a poet, scarred, keeps
scratching out words against paper
as if surfacing for breath.

The first time I saw these mountains
they terrified. The sun against snow
on their peaks so concentrated my eyes hurt;
the dark gouged valleys through which
rivers snaked, coiling through the join
the way desire brims in the blood,
surges in the legs and groin.

Today, as I fly over them, I am reading
Luminous Emergencies—its dark cry
for help, its disgust with sex.
Each poem slips me over its precipice.
I plunge once again into an abyss.

Word become flesh

Who is this man?
Chest-high in sky blue water,
half-exposed nipples
brown as the spots that speckle
his hand, which cups the liquid,
a flurry of drops as he raises it
catching the afternoon sun,
flames of candle.

Is his the face
the one that floats in the nave
of the country church
behind the shoulder
of the priest long ago who rattled
panes as his sermon thundered?
Bored with long-winded words,
I would sit
transfixed by the fresco,
the billow of beard, cobalt eyes,
full mouth, accepting God
had no body
until the Word
became Flesh,
His only begotten Son;
created like me
in His image.
I stared and tried to understand,
my own head attached
to a stocky body,
hands small as bantam eggs.

Or is he my father?
Each Sunday, his ritual
of rolling shavings of tobacco
into stiff white paper

he then seals
with a lick of tongue.
Those summers,
his body gliding
through waves at the lake,
skin white
as the bread in my sandwiches,
his pale fleshy arms
rising, falling
from view
as he swims
farther
and farther away
to the other side.

Or is he the man I met
by the Indian Ocean?
His body bore
down against mine,
skin soft
yet ridged with age,
fingers drawing such sounds
from my body
as if plucking my heart
through my mouth.

Or is he merely an imagining?
A man standing in frigid water
who wades
back and forth
while men glide
their luminous bodies
along brittle ice,
fall through cracks in the surface?
Each time one disappears
from view,
up through snow,
amassing at the lake's edge,

a torso rises
still as stone,
arms reaching out
tactile, beautiful
as marble

The stranger

1

A stranger is sprawled
across the bed,

arm flung over my leg,
foot curved around my head.

He is asleep.

Yet
in the darkness

his body full
of sound,

an underground stream
teeming with life.

Mouth expelling sharp blasts of air,
stomach rumbling,

a distant waterfall,
soft pops from his anus.

What else courses within his veins?

He arrived wired, a spring,

his small body
shaking at coming here,

wanting only one thing,
embarrassed

at his need,

how easily

I arranged it
over the phone.

His odour slightly sour,

ripe with traces
of sweat and oil,

and semen.

He moans, twitches
as if reaching out,

not for me,

for someone

not here.

It is always this,
behind shut eyes

the gap

between the person

we create

and the flesh actually held.

2

It spreads like ground fire

the burning

the longing
catching in the fine hairs
of the thighs.

Heat

trapped in the body

riddling

closed eyes,

fiendish images
drawn from primeval night

demon shapes,

illuminations

                    found

at the edges of vellum in hymnals
carved into arches of doorways.

And now this man
                    sprawled

the rise and fall of his chest
                    against the fluffed duvet

the beat of his heart
in the artery of his wrist
                    against my leg

building

the fire in my head

the ardour.

3

Purple as a plum,

stain of nectarine

on the skin

just above his rib.

A lesion? A lesion

I kissed it

as I did when an altar boy,
in humility
touching my mouth
to the stigmata of Jesus
each Good Friday
after the celebrant
removed
the mauve cloth,

the belief
through suffering
we are saved

4

Disease (dis-ease.)

me at this end of the bed
him at the other

estranged
from the flesh we held
momentarily

as if the expulsion
from the garden of our mothers' wombs

remains with us

our fingers aching,
twinning
for comfort,

the search for a man's hands

to deliver us
then pass us over.

Is it so
unreasonable?

this lack, this absence,

sweetening the pleasure of sex

only to fall
expelled

leading to

dementia

(dementi)?

closed eyes.

primeval night.

5

Shapes

at the edges of vellum,
in arches of doorways,

leper, cadaver, carcass

plague, pestilence.

a stranger sprawls
across the bed,

arm flung over a leg,
foot curved around the head.

It is all too simple.

life is life

and sex, sex;

suffering is suffering;
death, death.

In sleep,

the body
possesses its true self,

unashamed

of the dribble
of saliva leaking
from a lip fallen ajar;

and in death,

when reduced by illness,

it collapses into itself,
released,   a stranger

permitted one last organic function.

Stigmata

1

How I wish they'd quit asking.
Sometimes I'm hollow, their worries
wearing down my flesh, like the foot of St. Peter
burnished by constant stroking, the supplicant
seeking favour, absolution, asking after
my health, my mood, my weight, never asking
the question they are dying to ask:
when I got it and with whom. I want to shout
I'm the patron saint of fucking,
nailed with these purple stigmata
like St. Jerome, plagued by running sores,
lesions of long ago sins, retreating
to my cave, to silence, while the saved
praise celibacy. I am their warning:
what is possible, just one fatal
slip, bad timing, the wrong
person. Hell, it's not like the earth trembled,
an aftershock, or choirs of angels
sang us to our rest.

2

I wonder if she sees the irony or even
remembers. My mother, looking up
as she poured milk into cereal, her routine
phrase: "it'll be the death of you yet."
Of course she didn't know the truth,
only saw me distracted. Even I wasn't sure
what it meant, that phone call, the night before,
on my 16th birthday. How did he get my number?
Funny how we forget some things
while others cling, soggy grains
in a bowl, the rasp

of his voice in my ear:
"I want to meet you.
I've been watching you. I'm lonely,"
the cord around my finger, tightening,
the receiver's weight in my hand,
like my prick when I probed crevices
of my body, fretful something wasn't right.

Every night he called for a month until I gave in,
pulled to the restaurant as if by a thread,
an unwinding ball of wool, numbness
in my head and legs. I imagined
Theseus entering the labyrinth, drawn
to a dark chamber, an inner recess,
half-knowing it held
the real self, certain of the way back.

There he was, all grey hair and smoke,
smiling in a booth, an arm over the banquette,
casual as the scarf spilling from his open shirt.
All evening I avoided his eyes, but watched
his mouth, thick lips, tongue clicking
against teeth. Later, he passed me a joint,
the paper wet with his salvia, acrid
sweetness searing my lungs. I became
a balloon about to burst. His parting words
"I'll call," were fingers pushing
the hair away from my eyes.

He was a cunning man, biding his sweet
time, creating a hunger he fed bit by bit
to lure me back. One night, we sat
in his one-room apartment, lights off,
candle dripping wax, watching snow
filter through a column of light. His hand
held the roach like a wafer on my lips,
fumbled at my buttons, his tongue's sweetness
on my nipples, down the terrace of ribs, the snap

as my buckle fell open, penis
lurching free of my zipper.

3

At first, I went over every man
I slept with—the pickups in parks,
fuck buddies, friends I comforted in their grief,
who have since died. A desperate invocation,
a litany. Wanting an epiphany.
What for? Proof positive can't be undone.
I just want to get on with the little time
that remains, be fully alive, sick and sexual,
even if it is only dragging this heaviness
of bones to the window and feel the wind
stroke the ridges in my skin, like cock
thrust against the y-front of Calvin Kleins.

4

The virtuous things I have learned.
When I fell ill, like a child, I prayed
for this sickness be lifted from me.
Now I am resolved by the knowledge
I will be free when I die,
the remnants of my life little more
than myths taught or fabricated.

Was I so easy to read even then?
Did he know that once taken
I would lose my way, remain
here forever, alone in bed
twenty years later waking from a dream
of a man who stopped my breath,
held my hand as he led me
along the spiralling tunnels of a cave.
A stone rolled across its entry.
A burst of flames. Incineration.

Après *From The Spanish*

1

you, you have been dead
the heart a black hole
wanting
all skin and bones

you there
let some macho
give it to you good. with his gun loaded
what do you say to that?

he must have a fetish, this guy

heh, what's that you say?
he almost arouses you...why?

you can't get it up so you call
out...your voice dry leaves underfoot
crushed...in this poem, the dead speak

2

an invitation to darkness
ignites the air with darkness

the moon full...its face made strange

what does this say about love?
that dark mask
we all disguise, the face
we would wear if our right half matched the left

the man who has been pursuing the poet
the flesh of their torsos

the man is not immune...making love
he presses
thighs...wrinkles in the sheets

from the window above the wing of a jet
the Andes look like those sheets

the plane climbs higher and higher

the planet looks like some kind of platter
...staggering and huge as the moon...
it tilts in the hands of a drunken waiter

3

the space between stars
...not dead...but dreaming

electrodes
clamped to your penis

the space between stars
...not space...what is left of the body
...the pain

you dare not look
at the stamen of your penis

...man's hips...a shovel
to dig his own grave
your flesh conspires with the torturer
a premonition
makes you squint

you can't be
touched.

you have been debased.

4

why do I remember

believe poetry tells the truth?
...count on the poet,
          part angel...   part animal...
...whose words are secreted

from the glands....the shock of insulin...
the bite of adrenaline...nuances of estrogen

and testosterone
                    words formed by DNA.
...what we...feel...think...grace/ful and inter/weaving

5

after a night of rain
it is still cloudy but sunshine cuts through, razor-thin
the architecture...

                    a change of heart
you need a key
such a winding passage you wonder where
you are being led
                    to...
...spoken to in a whisper, an aside
a theatrical whisper...
you recognize its pitch
from the confessional.

in Greek tragedy
the dead...never rest.

night's blind

you are not here, and even
when you are, you are distant,
your body withheld

withholding, stifling
small cries, refusing
the pleasure points

of my fingers. the dark
thread, night's blind
behind which you watch

my voice wants
to fly up and scatter
in a smattering of words

like birds tearing themselves
from the skin of ice
but fear follows, fells me

fear of deficiency, of speech
or having spoken, the shunning silence,
the body after its last breath

the body once held and taken
into the mouth, now just skin
cold and unyielding,

concealed
loss of faith, faithfulness,
abundance abandoned

lashed by winter winds
white squall, the flurry/
wings pummeling, flight

where, where are you?
and why
these shards, disguised images—

a footprint rutted on a shoreline
an unmarked grave
a bird cleaved of its tongue?

Frangipani

Local lore names it
the tree of
loneliness.
And it is true.

Along the path through
the jungle everything
grows full
of itself. Rakes
of coconut palm
vaunt hairy husks.
Long
limbs of jade
vines curl
round fronds pleated
with petal.

But the frangipani
is always
solitary.

In a corner
of the yard
at the temple,
it is gaunt, shorn
as a monk
meditating
before Buddha,
its branches' gnarled tips
lustrous with flowers,
candles,
radiant with scent.

3.

Life is a Train

Each of us must stand in line,
wait for this journey to begin.
The scurry of hundreds of leather soles,
the thud of reggae music from a kiosk
against the concrete walls of la gare centrale,
irritates this random queue of bone-weary
businesspeople, shoppers thrown together
simply because it is time to depart.

In the narrow tunnel below each of us
settles into the confines of our seat.
A British boy faces me in camouflage pants and cap,
an ill-fitting man's tweed coat,
runs his fingers over and over the dust jacket
of Dostoevsky's *The House of the Dead.*
Beside me, a schoolgirl in uniform, reconjugates
the passé composé of the irregular verb *vivre.*
I rummage through my briefcase, retrieve
the *Selected Poems of Delmore Schwartz.*

The last time we spoke we argued about him.
Such a complex man. The promise of acclaim.
The fears that held him, consumed him:
sexuality, anti-Semitism, rejection.
I found him insufferable; you, more than the sum of his parts.
I thought of your mind, like phosphorescence,
trapped in a body that had not
worked since you were born.
I can't forget you at nineteen
passionate about Gide and Genet,
your laughter raucous at life's absurdity,
and the quiet despair.
Once again your summer would be spent
in hospital, just as each had been in your life.

Now twenty year later, the fight it took
just to keep going is over.
Your body finally has had its way.
I didn't even know you had been re-admitted;
never had the chance to say good-bye,
to tie everything neatly up, as if it were a poem.
I flip open the *Selected*, Schwartz's words leap out:
"How the false truths of the years of youth have passed!
Have passed at full speed like a train which never stopped."

Elixir

The windows wear death's crepe,
reflect back the light
in this room painted blood red.

Heavy gilt frames corbel
robust youth reclining by water.
A bronze warrior, slain in battle,
droops on a pedestal. Friezes
people the perpendicular of wall at ceiling.

In one corner, at a piano,
the musician's fingers fly
from the keys, unleash precise patterns
Bach caged in sound, frees them
into the air, a flock of birds
that pivots, reels, ascending.

I am uncertain,
whether it is ivory and wire
or skin and bone that releases
my wonder, this melody.

Later, among the well-heeled crowd,
in an oasis of cavernous room—
the walls an arrangement
of antique Arabian tiles—I query.
The pianist confides his thoughts were elsewhere,
the lumpy piano bench so uncomfortable.
What is this opulent fantasy
my need creates—a private retreat,
a masque resounding
against plaster and lathe,
deceiving both brain and heart?

People wander in and out
of the rooms, each so different,
yet linked by the man who designed it
according to his vision. He was like his house,
on the outside perfectly in keeping, but
on the inside appetite for plundering antiquities,
recreating the conceit of countries. 100 years later,
the house is rarefied, devoid,
except in subtext, of his desire.

I move among the guests as I did
through this city—a stranger.
Earlier tonight, my sole companion
the sound that rose up from my heels,
the scrape of leaves the wind tossed
as I walked along the Embankment.
The river's effluence disturbed
the buildings' reflection, dragged
them away until they were blurred
while empty coaches throttled
across Hungerford Bridge.

Here, in this city, in this room,
these close friends
mark the untimely death
of a surgeon devoted to virtuosity,
buffet his companion left behind.
We all move in this direction
—toward the absence each will become
through death or distance.
We carry these coaches,
this channel, these rooms, deep
inside our hearts,
ravenous for the elixir
of music and art, the restoration
of the body, as if it were still
possible to set the Thames on fire.

Easter Sunday (Boston)

A plume of steam rises from my teacup.
We sit at the refinished oak table
in a dining room built
into what was once a basement.
Rain fogs the solarium,
pools among flagstones of the sunken patio
where a shed once stood,
where iridescent shoots of leaf
break the arid twine of bittersweet.

Robert's fingers soak up the warmth
of coffee through the porcelain mug
as he unravels the pain of his childhood,
his family dissolving as he fled.
Remnants of his past,
swept into the corner of the garden,
like mortar from brickwork,
exposed now that winter has finally disappeared.

In the overcast afternoon
we sit at a concert in a museum
built to replicate
a XVth century Venetian palace.
Here a woman mourned for a child, then a husband,
spent years and her fortune
relieving the emptiness by acquiring beautiful things.

On either side of the Gothic fireplace, Belgian tapestries.
In one, Sarah wakes to the fire of life
bursting the cloister her womb had been;
in the other, Abraham arcs his knife
over the bound body of Isaac.
Above the hearth, enflamed in gold, St. Michael
pushes Lucifer toward hell while souls enter paradise.

Your body relaxes in the woven reed chair.
The musicians' fingers on frets,
their bows across tightened strings
ignite this musty room with notes
while outside magnolia blooms
flame on the ashen stalks.

Eclipse

Even in this distant city,
your illness, your impending death
darkens our conversation, our hands
like shadows covering our mouths as we are told
that the tumour has broken through your skin
the way the moon's plump cheek is pocked by craters.

I say nothing
recall a poem to your dying ex-husband.
And now you are caught in this obscuring.
What words have you for this passing into shadow,
you, who had finally found
your voice, also striken this way?.

Your tongue probes your mouth,
your finger circles the moles appearing on your skin,
you tell yourself fear is illogical.
Or, have you learned the strength of superstition,
the way ancient peoples were taught
the darkening hours of the moon are dangerous
and dyed their loved one white?

Later, we sit out in my sombre garden.
In a corner, a galaxy of nicotiania heavy with scent.
We watch the earth's shadow shutter the moon.
As if talk could keep its advent at bay.

The women claim the moon—
menstruation, fertility,
a woman with a basket on her back, a woman spinning.
The men quote Webster's—
eclipse: **from ek, out of + lepein, to leave**.

The moon slowly turns red, to shadow.
We are silenced
by this mystery darkness creates,
that words are fragile,
full of possibility yet limited.
We hope, like you, that laying them
across a white page renders them
fixed as stars that emerge
when light and dark collide.

In the White Giant's Thigh

Determined, the nurse draws the white coat
about her, the way I clasped my nightdress
that morning as dawn bled into the waters
trickling along the folds of the estuary.

So calculating, the doctor's needle slides
under the skin, effortlessly as Dylan
when a woman lies soft as sand beneath him.

How I hate what he has made me. He who writes:
"O Caitlin, my love, my Cat, my lovely love",
then spends his drunken self pummelling some bitch.
Legs up, feet in the stirrups, it's almost
as if, lying here, I am giving myself to him.
But the doctor is not here for that reason.
His hands run red as he hacks at the foetus.
It comes out bit by bit. Only three months to term.

"Was it a girl? Was it a girl?" I want to know.
He ignores me, a man going about his work,
diligent as Dylan dissecting thought and emotion,
stitching lines and rhymes with the thread of voice.

My feet are cold as that morning I crept
out on the sands at low tide searching
for fragments of his poem. The night before,
angry and jealous at its unmitigated conceit,
my hatred found scissors. My hands tore
through an open window, hurled
the work piecemeal into the dead of night.

The next morning I cradled the shreds, placed them
on the kitchen table as a token. I want to go
to America too. I am not a moral coward.
I want just a bit of fun. Mutely he swept bits
into his small white palm and withdrew.

Resurfacing

"I am hallucinating."
Having been through this
so many times you know
I'll recognize the clues.
The curl of your body,
foetus in an amniotic sac;
your fingers tight
as unopened water lilies.

"I am so tired of all this."
Eyelids half close
as you give into the fatigue,
simple struggle to breathe
weakening your body.

Your eyes are murky as the water
of the Ottawa River
I plunged into as a child.
Wlling to endure the soft flesh of bark,
weeds slippery as eels,
the plumbines of the lilies sunk so dccp,
snapping turtles with razor-sharp teeth,

just to prove I could swim
to the booms, that chained the bay,
and back, out of breath, praying,
desperate to reach the safety
of friends laughing on the shore.

Your eyes slide open.
Your lips move
a breeze troubles water.
I lean close, hear only
the clicking of tongue against teeth.

I, too, am tired of all
this, hoped I had left such dying behind
but it keeps resurfacing.

My fingers reach to outline
the ridge of shoulder through skin
as they did the edge
of boom in the water,
fear cold in my blood,
the slight tremble before
I plunged, turned back
to the distant shore.

Disappeared, presumed drowned

This has always been my medium,
Caught up in rhythm, ebb and flow,
Water filling my mouth.
All those years of poems
Recited against the ending of breath.

This sudden fire in my brain,
A state of reverie,
Images flooding consciousness,
The willing suspension,
The need to be one with them.

Washed up in my study, looking up
From the page on the desk,
Weary with writing, the scratched out
Lines and words, permitting myself
To be taken by the school of fish
Darting in and out of sunken trees.

In this element, I am mesmerized
By sunlight refracted in water. So clear,
The lines on the sandy bottom
As if my finger had furrowed them there.

A poet, I have learned. I must not
Struggle but give in. This is my calling,
My destiny to be submerged,
Released into the surge of this element.

Memory Box

My son loosens the elastic holding
his chestnut hair. A long strand tumbles
over his shoulder, onto his t-shirt, across
the image of the knock-kneed English boy
whose argyle socks ring his ankles. Underneath,
letters I can't see but know are there: SNFU
(Society No Fucking Use he has told me.)
My son's muscled chest and arms cradle
the acoustic guitar his dead mother
played when we first met.

We sit at the oak table
—him in boxer shorts, me in a bathrobe.
My son's fingers against vibrating strings
fill the hollow wood with resonant loveliness.
He is strumming his way through
Sunshine of Your Love, a song I heard
at eighteen when The Cream played
at the Capital, long ago pulled down.

Steam from a tea unfurls a curlicue in the air.
His music fills the quiet room
with such simple joy, such healing.
Autumn's wet cold wind lashes
against the window that, like a dam,
holds it, at least
for the moment, at bay.

You take down a tomato

It sits in your hands,
still warm from the atrium,
both of your palms flush
with the radiance of setting sun
at summer's height.
Curved, abundant flesh
against your chest,
held out to me.

I offer you this—
a poem, a knife
to unleash the swell,
wedges of crimson ardour,
the yield inside
its circumference of skin.

The cache of seeds
in our mouths
pungent and savoured.

4.

This bed an ocean

I am drifting drifting
in and out
of sleep
images   from dreams
clinging   seaweed
tussled in waves

your absence   stones
sewn into secret pockets
of skin
weights me down
dragged
into the depths

I have lived   with want
for so long
fatigue aching the muscles
the shore   a distant point
all hope   abandoned

and now   craving
for you   sharp
prow of an overturned boat
jutting out of the swell
just
beyond
reach

but still
trusting my heart
anxiety
propels me   life-long
the thought of you
a life line

Four Fetishes

1

I keep opening doors
rummaging among clothes
encased in plastic, searching
for someone lurking,
his knife drawn, held
by his hip, ready to lunge
up, crack open my ribs

I know he is there,
his breath jostles the hangers,
mice scuttle across the floor;
he has earrings,
piercings, a shaved head,
he is primitive,
a man hewn
from exotic wood,
to be left on an altar
in the deepest recess
of a cave

and his fierceness
fills my throat,
sounds without shape
—animal, guttural;
he is a child
banging my head
against a wall, the quick blood
deafening the pain
and I hurtle up
against darkness,
arms, torso pushing blankets
weighted as manacles;

and then always this
absence, craving
for shelter, for peace.

2

a voodoo priest
calls to the gods for healing
as his fingers embed
a small white egg
in the stomach cavity
of a fetish,
seal it
behind a lens of glass;
the fetish is so tiny, wooden, caked
in earth and webs and rust,
with spikes, triangles of metal
driven into arms, chest, back,
buttocks, legs, and groin; one ear
enlarged, half obscured by a clenched spear;
the other, as an ear should be;
the priest settles it
on an altar amid
bones, feathers,
a desiccated foetus.

3

beaten gold, beads of glass,
strung out to suggest luminous sun,
clutched in a white glove
held out
for the faithful, who on bent knees, behold
the host, white, round, opaque,
token for body blood,
simulacra of the piercing
of thorns and nails;
the faithful, certain that suffering cleanses,

sins forgiven,
throw down
crutches and braces,
rise up and leave behind
their aches,
their twisted limbs.

4

your hands are balm, sleek
over my thighs, curative as prayer,
but I crave more—
want you deep inside, random
memories stuttering through my brain
—insistence of fingers, tongues against lips—
until my body trembles
and craven sounds transfigure to words,
until doors seal up,
and I fall down finally
released, curl
foetal in my final shape.

Images, Tome 1

«J'aime presque les images autant que la musique»
(Claude Debussy to Edgar Varese)

1. Reflets dans l'eau

We are only permitted impressions
as the Docklands Light Rail
pulls out of Tower Hill,
past the sallow tenements
where, through a window, I glimpse
one man, arm raised, clutching
a tea cup while another turns
away. Your fingers staccato on my wrist,
point to the distance,
the autumn darkness clots, ink
stain against hundreds of lights,
festooning the mast of a ship,
the highest building in the British Isles
you say. I am only half listening,
my attention still snagged on that passing
scene in the kitchen. Had he set the cup
down on the table, the other man
just come in? Or, was he about to
pitch it, the other ready to duck?

The train glides around a curve,
lights at the water's edge
stitch the basin's loop. The cars stop
in the concave of station: Canary Wharf.
You lean forward, watch office workers,
collars unbuttoned and ties askew,
rush off escalators, push through opening
doors, cram into aisles, onto seats.
I think of the headlines back home
—these buildings almost sinking
a family whose fortune
shores up my country.

You recount how your ship docked here
that first time you arrived from Durban
to study, launch your career.
Even after so many decades
your voice betrays the liberty,
your feet pressing down
onto the gangway as it bowed
under passengers' weight,
the air brisk in your mouth,
your heart pounding, ignited
by desire as porters shoved
your steamer trunks into the boot
of an uncle's waiting car.

Your fingers beat against my knuckles.
Your voice fills the shape of my ear.
South Quay. We disembark
switch lines, go deep underground.
I follow you through
the doors onto the platform, let
you walk ahead through moorings
of light into shadow.
At eighty-one, you are still so elegant
your height full-drawn.
You turn toward me, your lips
discretely curve to a kiss.

2. Hommage à Rameau

I

The paths are rutted deep in the earth
as they arc, criss-cross unkempt grass
around the stands of oak on Hampstead Heath,
your breath ragged
as you mount a small incline.
It is not so easy as it once was.
You turn to wait while I catch up.

You speak of death,
as you have done several times
in the last few days.
Sometimes seriously,
sometimes joking, ready
with a scenario—a sudden
tumble onto Oxford Street
coming out from the Underground,
courteous shoppers pausing,
but not too long, weighted down
with shopping bags
they must move on. Never realizing,
I add, you once brought
London to its feet
in Wigmore Hall. So long ago,
you say. So long ago.

But today the music you made is invigorating
as autumn's air. The movements
of branches those notes
in the drawing room before we set out
as we listened to tapes of performances broadcast
across Europe, in Africa. I ask how you drew
these sounds from inside? What deep
recess like tap roots your fingers
reached? You smile at my imagery,
quietly say: «practice.»

I persist. Before you began,
did you fuse emotion to an image?
Did you follow the sheetmusic note-perfect?
Was it already arranged inside
your head the way you have memorized
every stop on the Piccadilly and Victoria lines?
You laugh. «There's talent, you know.
Occasionally inspiration.»

Over your shoulder,
along the Heath's edge, a white stallion
vaults over a fallen tree.
I think of the way my heart leaps
when I look at you, ask why?
The search for a father?
«Sometimes I just let go, follow instinct.»

II

You point the way
along the path, through a clearing
to the roadway, the house.
We walk side by side in silence,
past couples on benches unwrapping
sandwiches, thermos of tea. You unlock
the front door, we pause
in the vestibule uncertain
whether to go in or embrace here
in this enclosed space, unsure
what holds us together despite living
in different hemispheres, generations apart.

A low moan quakes your cousin's house.
The tube speeds on its way to Golders Green.

3. Mouvement

Belsize Park. Chalk Farm. Camden Town.
Tottenham Court Road to Leicester Square,
past Charring Cross and Embankment.
Our bodies sway with the rhythm of the coach,
the movement of our thighs this morning.
We touch and then roll away from each other.
The powdery scent of your skin on my fingers.
A tattooed couple in the seat across the aisle
watch us intently. His lips move to her ear.
A gloved hand covers her crimson mouth;

at her wrist, thick loops of chain spill out.
The two stand, leave. I watch your eyes
follow in their wake. We, like them,
believe the truth behind
what links us remains subterranean.

Each day I travel with you beneath this city
past stations with names I know chiefly
from movies and books—Knightsbridge, Earl's Court,
conjured images vague as waking dreams.
For you, they are the fabric of youth.
Disembark here, and just around the corner
the church where you staged your first recital;
or here, pass under the road,
two blocks down, the bedsitter you
and your first lover shared before the Blitz.

Is this us? This passing in and out
of view, distilled to remnants trapped inside
heads or hearts, reflections,
our faces in the window, thin
membrane that separates us
from dug out earth as we roll
onto Highbury & Islington. This station
we enter and then leave behind,
the route we have chosen
not so straightforward, emotion
close to hand as the folded map
I always carry, refuse to put away.
I trace and retrace our journey
certain only where we've come from,
wanting to anticipate but unable
to follow the conductor's voice
garbled through the speaker.

a delicate environment

your sweet tongue
along my thigh
circles the dark
stain of birthmark

what can I do to please you?

I want to say
go higher

if you only knew
when you pleasure me
what demons
float
in the nerves
beneath my skin

my birthmark
a bore hole
filled with
soft plug of silt

underneath
a labyrinth,
limestone chambers,
hot geothermal springs

and creatures
evolving
in a primeval world

albino
empty sockets
where eyes should be

a water scorpion
breathing
through a snorkel-like tube
a giant leech
colony of creatures
worms, snails, centipedes
scientists have yet to name

an entire ecosystem
a delicate environment

I want to say
go higher
but access is difficult

a cold rush of air
would drive
everything back
into my inner recesses

I want to say
go higher

be fearless

throw open
the hatch
on my subaqueous world

The Magician

Your hand on the wooden handle
Clutches the knife as if you were
A magician working the cards,
Shuffling, slicing,
Plump onion, tapered carrot,
Pungency thickening the air,
As segments, sections
Swell, sum greater than their parts
In the simmering stew.

Once I would have
Thought of murder, mayhem,
Only of the blade's edge whetted,
In your hand I watch
A two-sided blade that parses,
Blunt edge sweeping
Leavings from the cutting
Board into a cupped hand
That throws
Them into the pot.

At one time I would have thought
Finality and death
But now
Your hand on the wooden handle
Your skill with the thin edge
Of the blade speaks
Of nourishment, of sustenance.

The Carver

In this man's hands
Wood becomes liberated
From itself, shavings flying,
Ebony birds at dusk
Clattering in the concealment of a tree
Then leaping into the air,
Released over the veld,
A fine thread drawn through limitless sky,
Unbound from the comings and goings of those below.

In this man's hands
The heart of wood is unfettered.
The flow lines of its grain,
Unhindered by bark,
Now saturate the surface
In channels the rasp's teeth
Have scraped. Incised fibers
Smoothed and polished to sheen,
To a concise delineation
Of skin and bone.

In this man's hands
The wood becomes other.
Ochre of earth, midnight of wood ash
Rubbed roughly into pores
On forehead, nose, mouth and chin.
It becomes, after decades of weathering
By relentless sun, endless drought,
To stand ingrained. Now, through it
They become, released—their voices forged
Their limbs congruent in dance,
They, no longer boys but full-bodied men.

Acknowledgements

Eclipse is in memory of Bronwen Wallace; *The Magician*, You *take down a tomato*, *This bed an ocean*, *Four Fetishes* and *a delicate environment* are for Jamie Robertson; *Après From the Spanish* is with the permission of Mary di Michele; *Images, Tome 1* is for Glyn Townley; *Precipice* is for Mary di Michele; *Resurfacing* is in memory of Ann Marie Keeley; *Easter Sunday (Boston)* is for Robert Branson; *Life is a Train* is in memory of Randal Stanton; *Grosbeaks* was written for Ann Szumigalski; *Memory Box* is for my son, Aaron; *The Carver* was a parting poem for John Barton when he left Ottawa; *Elixir* is for the late Dr. Lionel Bowman; *Disappeared, presumed drowned* is in memory of Dr. Evelyn Voldeng.

Some of the poems have previously appeared in journals such as *Arc*, *Anthos*, *modern words* and *Prairie Fire*; and in anthologies, *Garden Varieties*, *Seminal*, *SugarMule*, *Written In The Skin*.

I wish to thank the various members of the Ottawa Poetry Group—Christopher Levenson, John Barton, the late Marianne Bluger, the late Diana Brebner, Ronnie Brown, Terry Ann Carter, Helen Humphreys, Nadine McInnis, Susan McMaster, Colin Morton and Sandra Nicholls who provided initial comments on some of the earliest drafts of these poems many years ago. My appreciation goes also to Neile Graham and Jim Gurley who also gave me insights into these poems and to poetry in general.

Special thanks to John Barton who edited this manuscript and who, like Anne, urged me to return to poetry.